A Very Good Guide
to raising a daughter

By Bill Good, The Father
and Jenny Good, The Daughter

Purple Box Press

This is what our lawyer made us say...He thinks he's funny.

The information contained in this book is provided in good faith, and every reasonable effort is made to ensure that it is accurate and up to date. The ideas and opinions expressed in this book are those of the authors. The purpose is to provide helpful and informative material on the subjects addressed herein. The author and the publisher are not rendering any medical, psychological, legal, financial, tax, holistic or any other type of professional (or not so professional) advice. If you do require such professional (or not so professional) attention, please consult with a qualified individual.

Furthermore, he advises that we need to state that we will not be responsible or liable for any loss, whatsoever, that may arise resulting from reliance on any information contained in this book or with respect to any information contained herein or any proposed answers, solutions, acknowledgments, comebacks, comments, water-cooler talk, claims, counterclaims, explanations, feedback, guffs interpretations, justifications, lip service, observations, quick fixes, not so quick fixes, rebuttals, remarks, quadratic equations, reports, resolutions, responses, results, retorts, returns, statements, wisecracks or thank you notes based on or arising out of the information contained herein.

So read this book at your own risk.

Needless to say, we adore our attorney's sense of humor.

Purple Box Press
12393 South Gateway Park Place
Suite 600
Draper Utah 84020

A Very Good Guide To Raising a Daughter

Printed in the United States of America

Purple Box Press and its logo, a purple box, are trademarks of Purple Box Press, LLC. Visit our website at www.purpleboxpress.com for information about special discounts for bulk purchasers.

First edition published April 2006.

Cover Design by Justin Mooney, Layout by Jenny Good

The Library of Congress Cataloguing-in-Publication Data is available.

ISBN-13: 978-0-9767768-4-0

ISBN-10: 0-9767768-4-7

A Very Good Guide

to raising a daughter

father

Table of Contents

Thank You *Very* Much!

Three people especially helped make this book happen.

Joava Good

She's the Wife and Mom. Without her, there would not have been a daughter, father of the daughter, and certainly no book about either.

Because she wanted another child, Jenny joined us and I received one of the greatest gifts a woman can give a man—being there when your child is born.

Mary Kay Office

Joava met her on a flight into Salt Lake. Mary Kay was the PR specialist who helped Richard Paul Evans touch so many hearts with *The Christmas Box*. She took his book from Xerox copy to mega bestseller.

And if you believe in chance, which we most certainly do not, it was that "chance encounter" that led to our meeting her. With her extraordinary gifts, we were able to bring the magic we had lived to life in your hands.

Su Falcon

Imagine the pressure of a deadline to get this book to the printer. Imagine the dismay when the camera-ready pages are discovered to be, well, non-existent. Imagine Jenny working `round the clock in panic to get the pages finalized. Now imagine her long-time mentor, Su, stepping in (uh, phoning in, actually) from 2917 miles away, calmly making suggestions, debugging software, and yawning words of eleventh-hour encouragement. Jenny graciously thanks Su for coming through in a pinch.

Any mistakes in the book are The Daughter's alone.

Joava, more than you will ever know, thank you.

Mary Kay, thank you for your wonderful light touch, your know-how and skill, and helping to make it fun.

– Jenny Good, The Daughter

– Bill Good, The Father

The Father on Families

Less than half of American families qualify as "typical"—Mother, Father and 2.3 children. If that's typical, the Good family isn't.

In our case, the kids are an "ours, hers and a neither's"... except they are all ours.

It started at a big party when I saw a pretty young woman in a long white dress and thought, "That's for me." I asked her to marry me the first night I took her out.

I knew she had a daughter, and not too long after we got together, Nicci and I had a talk.

I asked her if I could be her Dad. She thought about it, said "Yes," and I've been Dad ever since.

We formalized our father/daughter relationship some years later when I adopted her. But the decision was ours as we believe that family is not about biology, but about love, caring and responsibility.

Bret, the oldest, joined us last. He literally knocked on our door when he was 14 with no place to live. At age 14 he was working to pay his own way through a private school. Talk about our luck! He offered to trade room and board for chores. What a lucky day that was.

He created his own place in the family, first by becoming the older brother to Nicci and Jenny. Then later, when he was about to graduate from college, we asked him, "What do you want for a graduation present?" He said, "You're the only family I have. I want you to adopt me." And we did. He is our son as Nicci and Jenny are our daughters and each is brother or sister to the others.

So why is this story so much about father and one daughter when there are three kids?

Simple answer: we're the writers in the family. As Jenny began evolving into a writer, we talked of a project we could do together. This story began to tell itself. It's written for dads and their daughters in the hopes you can keep or recapture the magic of Dad and his little girl(s).

– Bill Good, The Father

Daddy's Little Boy?

I spent the months prior to Jenny's birth learning what I could about becoming a father to a son.

Sonogram technology was just becoming available, and we could have known we would have a daughter. But we were so convinced *she* would be a *he* that we didn't bother. From very early in Joava's pregnancy (OK, I'm old fashioned enough not to say "our pregnancy." <u>We</u> weren't pregnant. She was.) this was one rowdy fella.

So by 1976, I had three years experience as father of a daughter and felt I was doing OK. I knew I had missed out on three very important years. I knew I had already made some mistakes. I didn't want to repeat those with my yet unborn son.

So I read a bunch of books and frankly didn't get much help... oh, there were books on parenting but little on being a father and nothing on being father to a son.

So I talked to my father, my wife's father, my mother, and to friends who were fathers of sons.

I asked about what I should do and not do. Advice varied. But at the core of it was a notion of "rules."

My son would rather be beaten down than ever strike a woman. No bully would dare strike him because he would know how to defend himself.

I would teach him to be fierce in business and an aggressive negotiator. I would also ensure that he would have the finest education money could buy, even if that meant my wife and I worked round the clock.

My son would be everything he wanted to be, and I would help him in any way that I could.

His name would be Zane Williamson Good, Williamson after my mother's maiden name, also my middle name.

I was in the delivery room when I learned *he* was a *she.* As she eased out of the birth canal, I had a terrible moment. It looked like her skull was covered with blood. I feared some terrible birth defect.

"Doctor, what's wrong? His head!"

A second later, "It's just wet, red hair," he said. And then a second after that, "Congratulations, you're the father of a daughter."

He handed me a pair of surgical scissors. I cut the cord and he handed her to me.

I eased her in a body-temperature bath and washed her off with my gloved-hands.

And then something happened which cannot happen, at least according to what I later read.

At age 2 minutes, a baby cannot focus his or her eyes and certainly cannot smile. If she looks like she's smiling, it's gas or something.

But she did focus and she did smile. A thousand books can say it can't or won't or didn't happen, but that won't change what I saw, felt, experienced.

As I held her, she looked around, found my face, focused her eyes and gave me a smile that to this day lights up my life.

There was a fusion of spirits in that moment. No more thoughts of a son. I was the proud father of another daughter.

As I drove home from the hospital that night, I wondered, "Now what?" What about all those ideas for rearing a son?

I decided, "Nothing changes." The world is different than the one I grew up in during the 50's. I'll teach her all the things I would teach a son.

After getting into bed, the phone rang. A cold rush of fear hit as I struggled to find it. Something must be wrong.

It was my wife.

"Honey, she's screaming her head off. I really need some sleep. Will you come?"

I pulled on my clothes and drove back to the hospital. I walked into our room, and sure enough, Jenny was yelling.

I picked her up. She whimpered a minute or two and then was quiet.

I put her back with her mother, and she started screaming again.

I again picked up her and she quieted down.

For some hours, I held her and talked to her until she finally went to sleep.

I learned that night that she would have her own rules for me: Daughter's Rule #1: "When I call, you better come."

After we brought her home, there were many nights when she wanted her father. In time, when she cried in the night, I would just get up and not even wake Joava. If it wasn't feeding time, she wanted dad.

She called. I came.

It was probably not until Jenny and I started working on this book that I realized that one of the things I did right was allowing her to impose rules on me.

Since Jenny was able to exercise some control over me through her rules she did not need to revolt to gain her freedom and dignity. She had it. And then, after we'd screwed up, by further granting her freedom and dignity, it allowed us to get back together.

I mostly followed her rules and she mostly followed mine, and together we made it through as father and daughter and as best friends. Did everything work all the time? Of course not, but she did arrive at age 18 unmarried, unpregnant, and loving her family.

As the old saying goes, "Life is a two-way street." But only if you allow it and understand it must be that way.

Daddy's Little Girl!

If we weren't related, we probably wouldn't even be friends. But, as luck would have it, not only are we related, we are the best of friends.

Looking back, though, it may have come naturally to us only after some practice and some real understanding of the differences between us.

For example, I am your basic average, everyday all-American girl-next-door. I am nice and polite and helpful. I am that neighbor who will lend you a cup of sugar and not expect you to ever "repay" me. That's the outline, much like the outlines of images in a children's coloring book. And, yet, with my own flair I have colored outside the lines with streaks of my own intense independence, adding a dab of funky fuchsia next to the dribble of more conventional style.

I certainly colored in the attitude, style, behavior of the girl that I wanted to be, beyond the boundaries of the foundation that my parents provided.

Unfortunately (as much as I would like it to be otherwise), my experience of "discovering" who I am has not been that different than that of every other teenage girl.

Where I got lucky is that my dad was clever enough to learn from my self-discoveries, so as I changed, he did too. He watched while I painted the broad strokes of my life, studying my canvas as an art student would study a Monet.

When necessary, he was there providing some paint thinner, but even then he didn't take over or interfere. I was never punished for my efforts at growing up, even when those efforts got me into big trouble (when I needed him to be the most CALM, he was). The trial and error of my life became a journey to figure out where I fit into the whole picture.

By the time I had "figured myself out" he was still there, a friend, a father, someone I could talk to, joke with, laugh with, cry with. Someone I could trust.

This book is for every daughter who has ever tried to color outside the lines and was corrected for doing so.

Perhaps, with a little love, a few rules and some common sense, we can teach our fathers how to be better daddies. Then, perhaps through the process, we as daughters can also learn how to be a little more tolerant of our set-in-their-ways fathers.

In this guide, you will see some rules that may seem pretty obvious, but it was through the application of these common sense rules that my dad and I were able to survive the tumultuous teenage and young adult years and create an even better relationship now than when I was simply "Daddy's Little Girl".

Father/Daughter Negotiating Skills

Having trouble getting your daughter to do what you want? Defiant? Air between you thick enough to cut with a chain saw? Won't cooperate? Ignores her chores? You are sick and tired of... whatever.

Got news for you, Dad.

It's *your fault* because it's the relationship between you that needs fixing, not the dishes or her filthy jeans. At age 9 or 13, *she can't fix that.*

You could have but didn't.

The defiance is just her way to get back at you for letting slip the father-daughter magic.

So back off from today's battles. And maybe even lose a battle or two to preserve what matters.

Let's take the battle of the room.

I lost this one.

For years, I would launch an occasional assault on the way Jenny kept her things. Once I threatened to call in the University of Utah bacteriology department to see if there was a new strain growing.

Another time, I announced a new invention, "The Teenage Room Compactor."

She would be issued paper clothing, a large paper towel for a blanket, and a paper futon. Once a week, the Compactor would compress the contents of her room and eject it down the street. She would then be issued her new paper wardrobe, towel and futon.

Somewhere along the way, I decided to lose this one.

She had decided that life in a sty was fine with her.

I could have won by donning the all-purpose sermonizing robe and delivering a nearly endless parental harangue.

She would have hated me for it.

The price was too high. I wasn't willing to pay it. So I lost that battle, deliberately.

Mostly, we didn't go down that path.

Instead, we went from childhood through the "tween" years into teenage years without the defiance and bickering.

Why?

Because I stayed close enough to her to keep the relationship right.

In any relationship, each person has a mental laundry list of things he or she would like the other to do.

"Jenny, your room looks like a small army just decamped. Get in there and clean it up or I'm getting a shovel."

"Dad, pleeeeeeeeeeease let me stay up and watch..."

These issues and whatever you have going mostly sort themselves out by keeping the relationship right.

In younger years, the fix is really easy. It's a quiet talk, an unexpected treat, a walk. Later it's a trip to the mall, a conversation about something she's interested in.

Nurture the relationship and the normal give-and-take of two people who love each other won't be a problem.

And maybe, Dad, she has to win some of the battles you're fighting.

By letting her win some that truly don't matter, you can win the ones that do.

Jenny really clued me in on this.

I had been puzzling over why she was so cooperative. One night, sitting beside her bed, I asked, "Jenny, why do you do what I want?"

She answered with a slightly puzzled look that suggested I had asked a mildly stupid question, "If I do what you want, you'll do what I want, right?"

Righter than you know.

13

Daughter/Father Negotiating Skills

My parents had a few rules for my sister and me that didn't make any sense at the time. These rules were very hard for me to follow as I didn't get the purpose behind them. To me they were just silly arbitraries that my dad imposed out of fear. One of these rules was that I couldn't go to the Gully by myself.

The Gully was more of a mini-canyon than a gully per se. We called it the Gully since it's not quite as majestic as a canyon. But it was right across the street from my house and was full of things to explore. The opportunity to find Indian artifacts and build forts was incredible.

However, I wasn't allowed to go down there without an adult. The odds on getting an adult to accompany me to the Gully and really having fun building forts and playing Lost Princess were in the neighborhood of one in a million. So I broke that rule. Frequently.

Not only did I break that rule, but I also encouraged other kids in my neighborhood to break the rule with me so that technically I wasn't "alone" in the Gully.

Later after I had learned how to ride horses, I would take my friends and our horses down to the Gully. Again, another no-no.

This just seemed like a whole bunch of rules that made no sense and so I did not feel I needed to follow them.

Of course, I also knew that if my mom or dad found out that I was sneaking out of the house to the Gully, I would be so grounded.

I never thought to ask my dad exactly why I couldn't go down to the Gully. It was more fun to pretend that I was lost or running away. But he never told me why this was a rule. So I broke it.

The point of all of this is he had his reasons for wanting me to stay away from the Gully. It was (and is) a great place for a child to get into all kinds of troublesome activities. If a child screamed down there, no one would hear it.

But I wasn't so concerned with my safety back then. My only thought was that I had to get my dad to agree to let me go to the Gully so that I didn't have to do it *Mission Impossible* style anymore.

15

There were too many people who knew that I sneaked down there, which would surely lead me into trouble.

So without really understanding what it was that I was doing, I opened the negotiations. If I went with a group of three or more, could I go down?

That was my opening offer.

As long as there was an adult present was his response.

Well, crap.

If I went down on horseback with two friends, could I go down?

If there was a teenager with us.

And back and forth it went until I finally had what I wanted. If there was a group with four of us, we could go down on horseback.

Since that had been the objective all along, I was totally satisfied that I had gotten exactly what I wanted.

I finally had permission to go into the Gully and I didn't even need an adult with us.

My dad is pretty set in his thinking and it takes some coaxing and clever massaging to get him to relax his rigid rules, but it can be done.

The key to successful negotiations, though, is to know exactly what the objective is and then go for it.

Once you reach your objective, praise him and tell him how much you love him. Maybe even offer him a little treat.

My dad likes little jars of jam and honey. Find what treats your dad likes and make sure you have them on hand when you open your negotiations.

The Gully Negotiation was just one of many times when we've had to work out an agreement. As I got older, he relaxed his vigilance.

Life isn't so much about compromises as it is about agreements. When your dad really understands your viewpoint and position and can see that you won't be an idiot, then there'll be no need for a "compromise", he'll just relinquish more control.

Most dads want to do right by their daughters. At the end of the day, no father in his right mind wants to smother in any way that independent spirit of his little girl.

Once I asked my dad (I was a pissed-off 13 year old because I had to be home at ten on a Friday night) why we had to have any rules at all, such as curfews and whatnot, and he told me something that stuck with me.

"Jenny," he said, "My job as your dad is to make sure you make it to adulthood. I will relax the rules to the degree that you can prove you are competent and capable of being responsible for yourself. By the time you move out, I want to know that you can take care of yourself."

That night I set out to prove to my dad that I was capable and competent of taking care of myself and I didn't need supervision or silly rules.

And what I learned: He'll bend when I am ready.

But as daughters we have to be ready for the consequences and responsibility of having that control.

The #1 Rule: Be the #1 Man in Her Life

There is really just one rule for The Father: Be the #1 man in your daughter's life until she finds the man she will spend the rest of her life with.

All other rules lead into this one.

I didn't realize this at the beginning. I just wanted to be a good dad. But looking back with 20-20 hindsight, I can clearly see that the things I did were, in fact, intended to make me and keep me The #1 Man in my daughter's life.

The truth is: women need men in their lives.

Baby girls, little girls, teenage girls and young women need men in their lives.

That's the way the "game" is set.

For a married woman, #1 better be her husband.

And for a daughter, it must be the father.

#1 position is not something automatic. It is something you have to earn. You as sperm donor are just biology, not a father, not #1.

You earn #1 day in, day out, from day one when your daughter is born until the day she is married, at which point you will give up your #1 position to the man who must replace you.

If you are a jerk, never around, mistreat her, don't pay attention to her, you are not #1, and, I assure you, nature hates that vacuum with a passion.

If you let that #1 position slip just a little or a lot, some leering teenager (or worse) *will* slither into the #1 spot.

The #1 position exists whether it's yours or not.

But if you love her more than any man, become part of her life, bring her more joy and fun, pay more attention to her, talk more to her, teach her more, you will earn the #1 ranking.

But treat it as if it's yours only for a day.

To the extent that you, Dad, occupy that #1 position, she is surrounded with an invisible shield and is safe from the harm that boys and men can bring to a young girl.

She may think about sex, talk about it with her friends, want it, see movies about it, see it suggested on TV and pictured on the cover of every women's magazine, but if you're #1, you will, at least, have placed a massive roadblock in the way of males of any age seducing or abusing your daughter.

From that position as #1, you can influence her decisions without even saying a word. You don't need 64 lectures and 27 volumes. *There is just no room for another man in her life.*

This most important rule—Be The #1 Man In Her Life—will be fulfilled by faithfully following the other rules in this book.

19

If you think you have to use force or duress, guess what?

You're number 6000 or something. The #1 spot is vacant or some-one else got it.

Even if you once blew it and never created the #1 position, you can get there.

I don't remember exactly when I figured all this out. In fact, there may not have been a "when." Over time, I just came to the realization that "I'm the # 1 man in my daughter's life, and I'll give that number up when I'm good and ready and certainly not to someone I disapprove of."

As an aside, if you are fooling around or doing any of those things that lead to a divorce, you are destroying your family and will surely lose your #1 position in your daughter's life. It's a huge price to pay.

20

If you have already divorced, you now need to do everything possi-ble to regain your position. And remember, you don't get there by announcing it or acting like it. You get there by loving, talking, com-municating, teaching and, yes, enforcing a few common sense rules.

The #1 Man in My Life

Before you are allowed to read any further in this book you must ask yourself this question:

Do I want to play?

If your answer is yes, then you may continue. If you start to wonder what my question means, it means this:

Do you want to play?

I do not use the word "play" lightly. I have fun with my dad. We've never had a single fight. We've managed to solve every difference between us because we are both willing to play with this relationship.

We communicate through our different opinions. There are some things on which we will probably never agree, but these things are so unimportant at the end of the day because we both recognize that those differences are part of life. So why waste any breath on it when there are so many more important challenges to conquer. And there are so many more laughs to share and memories to create.

But the willingness to create it has to be there. And that's the key.

Just because my dad is *my* dad doesn't mean he is automatically assigned that position of #1.

I had to decide to give it to him.

He earned that #1 position when I was young because I was *his* number one priority (the whole family was). I knew if I needed him (or even just wanted to say "hi") that I could interrupt the most important business meetings, disrupt his working hours, visit, or call. Whatever I needed, I knew he was there.

This has *never* changed.

For that reason, and that reason only, I wanted him to have that position and so that is the position he occupies in my life.

Of course, I know it won't always be that way. I will get married someday and that position will change from my dad to my husband, but that man will have to have the ability to hold that position in the same way that my dad does and has.

But in that situation, it will be my willingness to play that game.

In the same way, it has been *my* willingness to play at this one.

So then the question, again, to answer is, "Do you want to play father-daughter?" If not, then this book isn't for you.

If you are happy with your current relationship with your dad, or if you don't really want to create the magic you shared when you were young, then this book is *definitely* not for you. And you should return it for a refund from your local bookstore or give it to a friend. (Don't send it to me as I will probably just send it back with a few suggestions.)

However, if you feel there is something more that you want out of your relationship with your dad, then this might be just the ticket.

The dance between a dad and his daughter is a very intricate pattern of steps that can go very wrong at any given moment. But if you're careful and have the desire and courage to see it through, this dance has the potential to be one of the greatest numbers you'll ever perform.

So ask yourself this question:

Do I want to dance?

Real Communication Rules!

When I googled "communication," I got 1,130,000,000 (as in a billion) hits. Googling "communication parent child" produced 32,700,000. Checking "communication father daughter" and we're down to a mere 13,200,000.

Key question: Does this Dad have anything to add to the information storm? You bet.

With this chapter, there are now 13,200,001 hits.

And mostly, Dad, you don't need those other 13 million theories and opinions. You need to understand how communication rules.

Communication with Jenny started early in the morning after she was born.

When I say, "We would talk," I mean that. If Jenny said "goo goo la la," I would reply, but not with baby talk. If I thought "goo goo la la" was a question, I might explain why it was raining. I answered with full sentences.

Communication isn't just talking. It's listening intently to what she is trying to communicate.

Once when she was a few months old, I was watching her as she lay on a changing table. She was moving her legs. Her face turned beet red, she kept kicking out, and then she started to yell. (She didn't cry much, but she yelled if she was angry or frustrated.) I could tell she wanted to move. I put my hand so her feet pressed against it. She pushed and scooted a bit. I moved my hand, and she pushed her way to the edge of the table. I turned her around and she scooted across to the other side. Back and forth she went.

So certainly communicating doesn't mean just words. Babies may not be able to talk. But they certainly can communicate. You have to look. See what she wants. Respond.

As soon as she started walking, we took lots of walks together. At the time, we lived in an apartment in Los Angeles, and we would walk very slowly around the block.

She always held onto my little finger.

On one of those walks, I decided I would help her communicate with the environment.

25

When we came to a tree, I might say, "Say hello to the tree, Jenny."

"Hi, Tree."

"Give the tree a pat." And she would.

"Say hello to the rock."

"Hello, Rock."

To animals, "Hi, Dog. Hello, Kitty."

Silly? Perhaps.

But you should see her talk to animals and tell them what she would like to have them do and then see them do it.

There was never a forbidden subject.

There was no *single* time Jenny asked about sex. Or drugs. Or alcohol.

We talked about everything. Today's tough subjects were simply things we talked about.

Sex? By the time Jenny was five, she had asked why the ducks over at the barn got on top of one another.

I certainly don't remember what I said, but I do know that I never showed or felt embarrassment. I suppose some parents might have difficulty with that, but I didn't. Jenny and I talked about what she wanted to talk about or what I felt she needed to know.

We might talk about politics, my business, capital punishment, elections ...and drugs. Whenever the subject came up, we would talk about it. Sometimes I would bring it up, but I always tried never to treat it as different from other subjects. And I never lectured, warned or threatened about drugs. I made sure she understood that they could mess her up for years, that they were illegal for good reasons, that horrible people sold them, and that they caused people to do harmful things to people they loved.

Nor were there ever certain subjects I discussed versus other subjects she spoke about with her mother. Sure, later on when her body changed and she started becoming a woman, she confided in her mother about girl things.

But especially early on, singly or together with Joava, we just talked about whatever Jenny was interested in. As boys began to enter her mind, I tried to put as much humor into otherwise serious subjects as possible.

So we had, for instance, "The Sequence Lecture."

It was a short one.

After having given countless variations of this lecture, Jenny might say, on her way out the door on a date, "No Dad. You don't need to give 'The Sequence Lecture. I got it."

My wife and I made a point of talking early and often. But we took great pains not to make drugs or sex or alcohol a topic of apparent special importance or concern.

While the talking never stopped, my first line of defense was to be so close to her I could tell if something was wrong. And it was only when I let up that vigilance by letting my #1 position slip that, predictably, a rodent crept in and drugs made a visit, though brief, into our lives. Jenny will tell you about that.

The Sequence Lecture

"Jenny, there's nothing wrong with sex. Or boys... well, maybe with boys. But there's nothing wrong with sex. But like a lot of things in life, it has to be done in the right sequence.

"First you meet a young man. Then The Father approves him. Then you go out. If you like him, you date. Then you fall in love. Then you go out more. Then he asks The Father's permission for your hand in marriage.

"If approved, you get married.

Then you have sex. *Then* you have babies."

27

Did those early walks talking to the flowers, trees, animals, and even the sky have anything to do with her marvelous ability to instantly establish communication with any person she chooses?

Most probably.

Always remember, "Nature abhors a vacuum." When one or both parents are gone, physically or mentally, something you don't like will fill that vacuum. Drugs. Sex. Gangs. Something. Be close. Don't permit a vacuum. Communicate.

Real communication rules. Not jabbering, yelling, lecturing, nagging or pestering.

Communication.

Talking to Dad

Sometimes I am surprised by how obvious this rule is and yet how fathers and daughters will ignore it!

I've never had any restrictions put on what I could and couldn't (or should and shouldn't) communicate about with my dad. Funny enough, when it came to the important things in life (sex, drugs and rock and roll) my dad was the first person I thought to go to with my problems, questions, concerns and curiosity.

When I got my first period, my dad was the second person I told (after my mom, of course). We all had a good laugh over the fact that it happened in my white riding britches.

Because of the fact that I never sensed any embarrassment from either of my parents about any subject, I never learned to be embarrassed by any kind of communication. For this reason, I have never felt uncomfortable talking to my dad about anything, whether it is sex, drugs, smoking, drinking, world politics or philosophy. On some things, we disagree—mostly due to generational differences. On others, we have a similar mind—I am my father's daughter after all.

I find that this idea puts me in a very small minority of girls. Who knew?

This is largely my dad's fault, this openness between us and I hold him completely responsible for making me even that much different from the rest of the herd.

He did something that I hope I will be able to do when I have my own children. He made it safe for me to talk to him about anything.

It goes back to an early agreement between us. It started with a lie actually. A very terrible lie that I can't believe I even tried to pull off. But as children do, I lied, got totally busted and got my one and only spanking.

I didn't ever want to go through another spanking ever again. It sucked. I was humiliated and while it didn't hurt that bad, it made me feel really ashamed. I knew there had to be a better way than that. And so there was.

So good. Decision made. I was going to be a "good girl" (Ha! Fat chance of that!) and never get spanked ever again. I never did get spanked again, but I certainly didn't quite manage the "good girl" part in its entirety.

While my intentions have always been good, I have an avid lust for adventure fueled by my insatiable curiosity about life. It sometimes has gotten me into minor trouble. Let's just say that I've never been arrested. I am lucky. Thank God.

I think on some level my dad realized that no matter how hard I tried (or how hard he did) I was going to get into things—good and bad.

Anyway, the situation that led up to The Lie (and subsequently The Spanking) was so silly that like most childish actions it makes no sense.

I had a beagle, Sadie. Every night before shower and bed, I had to take her outside and make sure she went potty before we put her away for the night.

Honestly, the dog was a pain in my six-year-old ass and I didn't like taking her out. Especially at night. When friends were over. She would run away or howl or take FOREVER to find a spot. I had a girl-friend over that night and we were mid an intense Barbie Marathon when I got the knock on my door and the order (via my sister) to take the dog out.

I tried stalling. I tried to pretend that I didn't hear my sister through the door. I ignored the intercom. I tuned my mom out when she called upstairs. Finally, my dad knocked on the door and told me to take Sadie outside, then it was off to bed for me.

I dragged my feet all the way outside. Sadie was even less inter-ested in going outside than I was. But outside we went. I waited what I thought was a respectable amount of time, then went back inside, both Sadie and I excited to get back to our games.

Apparently I did not wait long enough, because not two seconds after coming back in to the house my dad asked me if she really went to the bathroom.

Then there it was. The Lie.

"Yes, Daddy. Sadie went pee outside."

"Really?" He said. "Show me."

Uh-oh.

Okay, no worries. I took him by the hand, led him outside, and pointed to a spot <u>on the sidewalk</u>. I mean how idiotic was I? There was no wet spot. I realized that just in time and corrected my lie to the grass next to the sidewalk.

31

Unfortunately for me, my dad was one step ahead and knelt down on the grass and felt it before he asked: "How come the grass isn't wet?"

As quickly as I could (but not quickly enough) I tried to come up with a plausible excuse.

"Did you lie to me?"

Busted. I nodded, in terror that I was going to be fed to the neighbor's dog or worse grounded from Barbies for life.

Back inside we went, past the guests, up the stairs, into my room. He sat me down on the bed and explained something about lying and spankings and what not, but I was too terrified to really remember what he was going on about.

The next thing I knew I was bent face down over his knee. One stinging smack on my butt and my whole world was over. I think I blanked out at that point for a few minutes because the next thing I remember is sitting on my bed and hating my dad so vehemently that if I could have hurt him in some way, physically or mentally, I would have done it.

The Spanking didn't hurt. It was the punishment factor that did me in. I don't know how long I sat there on the bed stewing before my dad knocked on my door to apologize.

He came in and sat down next to me. I scooted away from him and refused to speak.

I didn't sit silent for long before I launched into a tirade of hatred against him. He didn't take it personally. I don't remember what I said or how he responded, but what I do remember is that he confessed about hating The Spanking as much as I did and he NEVER wanted to do it again.

That was when he asked me why I had lied to him. I told him that I didn't want to be in trouble because Sadie wasn't going to go potty. And I didn't want to be outside anymore. It was cold.

After several minutes of silence, he offered me a deal: He would NEVER get mad at me if I confessed to troublemaking first. However, if he had to find out on his own there would be Hell—spankings, groundings, and loss of privileges.

I thought that over. It sounded pretty reasonable. It was something I could do so I agreed. We hugged.

That agreement between us established a real openness that has never gone away. From that point forward, there really wasn't anything that I couldn't talk to my dad about <u>and</u> vice versa.

This wasn't that big a deal when I was little, but it was big when I became teenager because I got in trouble. I smoked, I drank, I dabbled in drugs, I spent too much money, I wrecked two cars (before I learned to drive and had a license), and got myself into a slew of other mischief.

33

And apparently since I've *never* been a good liar, I was forced to keep that promise to my dad even when I really wanted to hide what I had done. And, believe me, I tried a few other times to hide some of my mischief (I took my parents' car, totaled it, and blamed the nanny) but those are different stories and I confessed before either of my parents found out the truth. Really, though, the lie compounded the action and it was the lie that made me feel terrible.

So, yes, I got in trouble with the parents. I pissed them off, but, ultimately, since my dad had made it so safe for me to talk to him, I could go to him, fess up and didn't need to lie to cover up what I'd done. (His response to my crashing the car? "Well, at least, the air-bag worked.")

By giving me the opportunity to confess, he taught me to take responsibility for my actions. He taught me how to keep a promise. He taught me that communicating (and telling the truth) is so much easier than trying to hide from the possibility of what could happen.

Most importantly, though, I trusted him to keep his promise.

And he did.

In later (and more responsible) years, this principle has translated itself into a really easy friendship, filled with a lifetime of inside jokes and funny memories.

I don't bear the scars from those years that most teenagers do and I'm pretty sure that my dad is largely responsible for helping me through that time.

If your dad is not well-versed in this fine art form, then teach him how to do it. Start slowly and tell him something that'll shock him a little, but won't give him a heart attack.

He might freak out. If he does, remind him that is NOT what you two agreed and if he wants you to trust him, he has to maintain his side of the bargain.

If he doesn't freak out, then good job.

It's not easy fessing up to your crimes. At first. But it does get easier as you get used to it.

And the more you confess, the easier it does get. But again, you both have to be willing to go there, stay there and get through it.

Good luck!

A Safety Net:
Independent, But Never Home Alone

Don't even think about teaching "stranger danger." As she gets older, increase your vigilance and your creativity. To teach anyone to be afraid of strangers is to teach them to fear people, a terrible lesson.

The first duty of a husband and father is to keep your family safe. Let down your guard just a little, as I did when I was focusing on some business matter or other and not talking to Jenny as often, and the price you pay can be beyond calculation.

The art of keeping your children safe, especially your girls, is to keep them safe without teaching them fear.

Obviously, I could have kept Jenny safe by telling her what a dangerous world we live in, teaching her to fear strangers, and never letting her do much of anything.

To keep Jenny safe, we evolved three strategies:

1) Don't let dangerous people near, but don't let her know she's being protected.

2) Always know where she is, what she's doing, and who she's with.

3) If her car, house or anything else she's involved with is unsafe, handle it no matter how old she is. She's still your daughter. You're still her dad. "Keep her safe" is one of your duties so long as you breathe.

After our move to Utah in June 1980, we built a house in what was then a semi-rural part of the Salt Lake metro area. I cannot even remember discussing with my wife that we might allow her to be home by herself. Though the Salt Lake area is a highly religious community and probably safer than most, Ted Bundy, the serial killer later executed in Florida, had included Utah in his murderous rampage.

So we would no more have discussed allowing Jenny to be unsupervised than we would have discussed bringing snakes or rats in for pets. Nor was there ever a possibility that she might walk or ride her bike to the barn where she kept her pony. It was less than a mile away. While Jenny did sneak off a few times, it was not often.

If she needed or wanted to go some place, one of us just took her.

Alone in the house? Not a chance.

Friends over? Sure, when there was adult supervision.

When she came home from school, one of us, or our older daughter or son, was there.

Years later, when I explained the effort we put into insuring her safety, her mouth hung open.

"I had no idea," she said.

That was the whole idea. She never knew we were concerned about her safety and never learned to fear the world.

When Jenny was 16, we agreed to let her move to Southern California to seriously pursue equestrian show jumping. Jenny is a very good athlete.

How to keep her safe?

For Christmas, my wife had given me a German shepherd. I named her Greta Garbo Dog because she was incredibly beautiful, as was her namesake. She and Jenny instantly bonded, and an idea began to evolve.

Certainly, it was unacceptable to send a 16-year old girl to Southern California unchaperoned.

Solution: Greta became her chaperone.

So Jenny and I made an agreement. Wherever she went, Greta went.

And I slept better knowing if anyone tried to hurt Jenny, Greta would kill them or die trying.

Jenny told me that once a couple of unsavory types headed over to her car when she was filling it with gas. Greta, who had an uncanny ability to sniff out what I call "unauthorized persons", sensed something not OK, jumped off the seat and stuck her face, complete with pearly whites showing, out the window. The young men, who undoubtedly had impure thoughts surging through their tiny minds, screeched to a halt and headed back wherever they came.

And then later, Jenny and Nicci decided to share a house together. They had some boxes in the back yard. A big guy in a black hood decided to help himself until Greta nailed him. He went running down the street with Greta snapping at him accompanied by Nicci's beagle howling loudly enough to wake the dead.

Good job, Greta. Well done on waking the neighbors, Lucky.

Hardly a month goes by when I don't see some silly, stupid story somewhere about how our darling children don't have time to play

37

because they have too many dances, soccer games, gymnastic meets or whatever events to attend.

What nonsense! If they need time to play, they'll tell you. But if you're doing your job, they won't have time to get in trouble. "Idle hands," as the old saying goes, "are the devil's workshop." It's when kids don't have enough to do and don't have a parent who cares enough to make sure they have plenty to do that they go where they shouldn't and do what they shouldn't.

Part of our strategy for keeping Jenny out of trouble was keeping her so busy she didn't have time to get into trouble. And if we had planned the activities, we would always know where she was, what she was doing and who she was with.

You've probably heard of what's called the "Peter Principle." Some management consultant coined it.

"Work expands to fill the time available."

Not exactly true with kids.

"Bad stuff expands to fill the free time available." For a lot of years, there was just no time available for the bad stuff.

She went to school. Then went to the barn. By the time she got home after riding, mucking the stall, taking care of her horse, she was one tired girl.

Expensive protection!

Horses are a giant, industrial-strength, money-pump performing first class depletion of parental assets.

But why do you work?

To bring up your daughter so she arrives safely at young woman-hood, not having been pregnant, drug free, and loving her parents.

Your job, Dad, is to do whatever it takes to find something she's interested in—or, at least, will do—and then make certain she fills the time available with schoolwork, sports, church, approved friends (many of whom she meets through sports), and family outings.

When she's involved in a sport, you will always know where she is, what she's doing and who she's with. "Teen-age insurance," I came to call it.

Trust Him to Bring You Home

In this chapter, you are going to read about my crash course in self-destruction.

You might wonder, "Why do I want to follow these rules? These people are nuts!"

But amidst all the misery and trouble that I caused during this stage in my life, there was a lesson we both learned. Perhaps this was the defining moment of all our hard work from when I was younger. This was the moment when our relationship was put to the test. Would we be strong enough to survive?

In some families, it is these moments in time that rip the family apart and they are never quite the same afterwards. Mistakes in life do happen. It's all part of learning how to get along in this world. And it's not always easy.

So while this book focuses mainly on the things we did right, it would be neglectful on our part not to talk about the times when we also went wrong.

And we did go wrong. On both sides mistakes were made.

However, because of all the groundwork that was laid down when I was much younger, it probably saved my life, and so I think it deserves a mention here since the relationship we created early on pulled me up through the darkest times of my life and back into the light.

My dad's faith in me and love for me picked me up when I fell on my head. It wasn't easy. It wasn't funny or taken lightly (though it might seem that way sometimes in this book). It was my dad that pulled me back from the brink of collapse.

Even when he was hundreds of miles away, the bond we created between us was still strong enough to keep me from diving head first off that proverbial bridge.

41

At that time, my dad's power as #1 was somewhat usurped by my boyfriend. My dad and I weren't talking very much—it was the only time in my life when we didn't talk every day. I was definitely asserting my "right" to be grown up. I was an adult after all. I didn't need my daddy anymore.

So there I was, all of nineteen years old, living on my own in California, riding horses competitively. And I was good. I had a boyfriend, a house on the beach, a great life and I was happy.

A lot of the kids I hung out with did drugs—whether they were legal or street. I thought I was really lucky in that most of my friends thought it was super cool that I had never done drugs. I was the anti-drug poster girl lecturing my friends about the stupidity of doing drugs. Not that it made any difference at the time.

My first contact with drugs came in the form of a practical joke. My boyfriend loaded a cigarette with hash and gave it to me. I smoked it.

It wasn't until my roommate freaked out and went after him trying to find out what mischief he had caused that he confessed to the dirty trick.

I was devastated. I lost my soapbox as the anti-drug girl. I don't have any answers or justifications as to why I didn't just dump my boyfriend and all my friends at that point and start over. On my dad's side, he didn't really know where I was, who I was with and what I was doing. Obviously.

But I do remember thinking that night that my life, as I knew it, was over. I could never be part of my good, upstanding family anymore. They wouldn't want someone like me. Stupid thoughts brought about by my own wrecked personal integrity.

The first time I really got high, I walked around in a daze in a small circle for hours. Then I went to some fast food joint and consumed three double cheeseburgers and two large cokes. I couldn't even feel how full my stomach was. It was a little terrifying.

And so began my downward spiral.

I smoked pot just a few times (seven to be exact), but it was enough to utterly destroy all the self-respect and integrity I had spent my whole life building up. I can chart my life sliding out of control from that moment to what I call The End.

Over the course of a few months, my entire life fell apart. I broke up with my boyfriend, my horse got permanently injured, I blew out both my knees and was drinking way too much for someone who wasn't even of age yet.

I was living a life that was so opposite to everything that I had been raised to believe that I didn't know if I would ever be able to recover my true sense of self. I had become everything that I had hated about this druggie culture of my generation. And I didn't know how to get out. And this is where all those rules, so carefully tended to when I was young, came through and pulled me back to safety.

Though my dad was eight hundred miles away, I knew that if I had the courage to go home, he could and would help me.

At the rock bottom point of my life I was living in my car (and had been for about a month) with my dog and all my stuff. I knew it was time to go home when I took "my house" up to visit a friend (so I could shower and sleep in a bed). He lived about a half hour away from where I was. I started driving and by the time I got to his house, I couldn't remember how I got myself there. Literally, my entire drive to his house was wiped from my memory as though I hadn't been there for the experience.

There was no memory of those thirty minutes. There still isn't any recollection of it. I might as well have been transported.

I drove right past his house and kept on driving until I got home. I called my sister (as my parents were on a trip at the time) and told her to wait up for me.

I drove all night to get home and, as promised, my sister was up.

43

It took me a week to get up the courage to confess to my sister what I had been doing. She promised that she would be with me if I needed her to be so when I talked to my parents about it. Nicci further promised me that everything was going to be fine and that I simply needed to trust mom and dad to be there.

My parents got home shortly afterwards. Since I had already made that first momentous confession to my sister, I wasn't so worried about the ramifications of the next confession. So I went for a walk with my dad and told him everything.

I told him about how I was a loser who was homeless; I had destroyed my credit and couldn't pay my bills. My horse was never going to recover and I was going to have to have knee surgery. My life looked bleak. Really, really bleak.

His response to all of this: "Thanks for telling me."

Then: "So what do you want to do?"

My answer? I want to start over and figure out what I am supposed to do.

He then suggested that first I stay home for a bit and we make a plan. Then when I was ready to go back and conquer my California "demons," he would drive back with me and help me find a place to live.

I stayed home for about six weeks before I was ready to go back to California. Together my dad and I drove to San Diego. He got me settled in a boarding house filled with foreign exchange students. It was incredible. Here were people very different from the insulated horsyworld that I had been living in for so long. I actually was able to talk to people about things other than horses and the next horse-show.

It was a gradual way to get me back on my own. Alone, I probably would have lost it again as I didn't have it all together yet. But in this house full of people, I was never alone to dwell on things that could get me in trouble. I was no longer drinking myself into oblivion and the drugs had stopped completely.

After a month or so, I was ready to get my own apartment. Mom came down and helped me find and furnish a place of my own.

Slowly with both my parents behind me, I put the pieces of my life together again. I went back to school and tried to figure out where I was going and what I was destined to do.

That time was the worst part of my whole life, and yet, in a sense, it turned out to be the best thing that ever happened to me.

Today, I am healthy, happy and I have a job that I love with my whole being. Through all of it, I found God and faith and a sense of myself that had never before been defined.

And the foundation of all of that experience came from knowing that no matter what I did, I could always go home and my dad would always be there to help me get through whatever I was stuck in.

I haven't had a drink in years—not because I was an alcoholic and couldn't control the impulses—but because I don't need it or want it. I don't do drugs and haven't since I was nineteen. I don't smoke (anymore). Things are good.

Brilliant, actually.

Make Learning Fun

From as early as I can remember, the most important thing in my life was learning.

Both my parents were readers, and a high point of my life was getting a card to the adult section of the library when I was about 8 years old.

I wanted Jenny to feel that same burn for knowledge I felt.

At a minimum, I felt I could make learning fun.

So when I read to her, I acted out the parts, provided full sound effects—roaring bears, clucking chickens, barking dogs or whatever.

I spoke in different voices—Papa Bear was basso; Momma Bear, contralto; and Baby Bear, soprano. My frustrated "inner actor" leapt out and had his moment on center stage—most nights when I was home and many nights when I would call in from a business trip.

The unstated lesson was: All this magic comes from books. But here's the important point, Dad. Knowledge you can get from books, but a teacher communicates the love of learning. My job, your job, is to communicate the love. I did that with our nightly theatre.

There were times when I thought the lessons hadn't worked. Until Jenny's mid-teens, I saw only flashes of talent, kind of a lackadaisical attitude toward school and books.

Then, suddenly, the seeds sown so carefully in her early childhood burst out in a glorious thicket of color. She finally discovered reading and learning.

Once in later teen-age years, I remember telling her, "Jenny, we're going to watch a movie. Do you want to join us?"

"No thanks, Dad. I've got a book."

47

From Pupa to Bookworm

As a little girl, there were things that were VERY important to me. One of those things was Storytime.

I don't recall when I decided Storytime was a rule, or even if I consciously made such a decision, I just remember that it was an all or nothing situation, and the 'nothing' of that part was just not allowed.

I *demanded* that my father read me a story every night before bed. It wasn't so much a request as it was a requirement to my own well-being. I *needed* Storytime every night.

Aside from the obvious benefit of spending quality time with my dad—something quite hard to come by when he was building his company from a one-man operation to the corporation it is now—Storytime pushed me gently on a path that I would eventually walk on my own.

Thirty minutes with my dad at the end of every night opened my imagination to the possibilities that I otherwise would have missed.

Like all children, I was insatiably curious about the world. I wanted to know why the sky was blue, why the stars were so far away and why couldn't I have some in my room, and what do dogs really think about? Most importantly, I wanted to know how come the grocery store had doors that opened as if by magic, but our house did not.

Each night, my father would satisfy my ravenous curiosity when he let me disappear into a magical part of life that I didn't even know existed.

I became part of the story, a character involved in the plot to free America from English rule or an observer peering through the telescope of Galileo's discovery and seeing that the Earth *wasn't* the center of the universe.

I painted the Mona Lisa beside Leonardo Da Vinci and lay on my back beside Michelangelo as we put the final coat of fresco on the Sistine Chapel. I ran away from slavery with Harriet Tubman. I spent every night I with someone new.

When I later studied these same historical figures in school, they never held as much fascination as they did when my dad brought them to life.

In addition to stories about historical characters, he created a fantasy universe with an evil cat, heroic lion, friendly snakes and a tiny creature called a "Nouse." Two or more of them were "Nice."

The cast of characters included Nicci Nouse, Jenny Nouse, Sneaky the Snake, Meany the Lion and Mouseford the Cat. My dad invented the "Nice" family suspiciously like my sister and me, who were, of course, part of the "Good" family.

Every new story started with "The Nouse Song" which we would sing at the top of our voices. To this day, I can hear the voices and smell the scents of Jenny Nouse's "little house in the forest, with lions and tigers and bears all around."

At some point, I must have concluded that Storytime was one of my rules. I demanded one every single night. Many times when my dad was traveling, he would call in with one. I craved the opportunity to slip into the past or into the fantasy world he created and watch the miracles that unfolded with every new discovery.

It was freedom to experience the history, the future, the magic of other worlds.

50

It wasn't until I started writing professionally that I realized exactly what my dad had taught me with Storytime.

By the time I was in second grade, I knew more about history than any of my other classmates. We'd had an assignment to give a six-minute oral report on one of our heroes—someone who had made a difference in the world. My report focused on the Storytime selection I was reading with my dad: Louis Pasteur and the rabies vaccination and pasteurization. I was teased by my classmates for weeks afterwards for being a nerd, but I couldn't have cared less.

I was learning without even realizing I was being taught. And it paid off tremendously when I later discovered a desire to tell stories.

I started to write a story called "The Dollhouse." It began as a description of *the perfect dollhouse*. Every detail I created was something that I could see in my mind, so I wrote it down and sent it to my dad. It was the start of building our incredible relationship in a different direction because my dad had discovered something new about me, and I discovered something new about him.

Then one day, I emailed him an entire chapter of "The Dollhouse."

He wrote back telling me to send him more.

As we wrote back and forth, he realized that I was actually *not* the intellectual airhead that I tended to portray. It surprised him, as it surprised me that he became so enthralled in the story I was writing. He again put on his hat as a teacher and guided me through the process of keeping the story on track and well researched. He helped me develop my style of writing as an art form, and he kept me going when I got so frustrated that I wanted to cry.

After a few chapters, he told me, "Jenny, if your teachers could do what you can do, they would be writing not teaching."

51

He offered me a "scholarship," which meant that he would support me for a year if I met his terms—writing, writing, writing 10 hours a day, six or seven days a week. I have never worked so hard in my life.

"The Dollhouse" evolved into "A Hero's Welcome," a story of a little girl and one of the great hero's of World War II. It's a thousand pages, and I'm now going back through it to get it ready for publication.

I had a goal to finish my book, and that is exactly what I did. With my dad supporting me every step of the way, and cheering me on, I began to understand that he was so much more than a father.

My dad has been my teacher, my mentor, my confidante, and most importantly, above anything else, he is my friend.

When You Are Laughing

Ok, you've heard it five billion times: Laughter is the best medicine. Not only does it cure, it is a preventative. It prevents grouching, yelling, cursing, force, threat and on and on.

I have no recollection of doing anything other than wanting to make her smile and laugh.

OK, OK. She would do things that annoyed me. But that's not where I focused. "Water off a duck's back." "Don't make a mountain out of a mole hill," etc. etc. All good advice.

Focus on the good. Mostly ignore the bad.

If you're laughing, you're not doing anything else, like being mad at each other, or yelling or chewing each other out. Laughter is so much more fun. As a matter of fact, an early title for this book was, "Laughing Out Loud (LOL): The Rules for Fathers and Daughters."

Maybe she started it with that first smile that lit up my life from that day forward.

Laughter is a theme of our relationship. Today, we keep an instant message link open and frequently chat back and forth. One of us will say something that gets a laugh from the other. The response is inevitably, "LOL."

When Jenny was a tiny baby, I made silly faces and had a full menagerie of animal sounds.

Then exaggeration. What a hoot that was…and is.

I remember once getting my head really close to hers, perhaps to give her a kiss or nibble on her ear, and she pushed me away. I completely exaggerated the effect of her little push and propelled myself across the room into a chair.

She shrieked with joy.

Once, when she was about four, we were walking into a grocery store. Just before we would have stepped across the electric eye of the store, I snapped my fingers, and the door opened.

She looked up at me in awe, and then immediately caught on. "Dad," she said with mock sadness. She was on to me early.

One Christmas, when shopping in a mall, we walked past a Hickory Farm stand with a big display of 3-foot sausages. I grabbed one and assumed the "en garde" fencing pose. She stalked off in embarrassment.

Later that same day we were at Blockbuster renting a video. The sales clerk had really curly hair. I asked her, "How do you make your hair so wrinkled?" Jenny again stormed away in embarrassment.

I realized I had gone a bit overboard, and so when we got in the car, I told her I thought that she deserved a serious dad and that I was being entirely too silly. I suggested we each pledge to be serious, not silly. So we drove down the road scowling…until one of us cracked up.

A lot of our silliness happened in the car, when it was just the two of us.

And then there was singing.

We started with "What does a duck say?"

"A duck says 'quack'."

"What does a kitty say?"

"A kitty says 'meow'."

"If a duck says 'quack',"

"And a kitty says 'meow,'"

"Then what does a little doggie say?"

Soon I was messing with the lyrics.

"What does a duck say?

"A duck says 'meow'."

"No, Dad, a duck says 'quack.'"

When we would get into the car to run an errand, we weren't just running an errand, "we were off to see the wizard..."

Then later, when she was learning phonics, "We're off to see the liz-ard," which, since kids seem to have a natural sense of correctness would earn the rebuke, "Dad, its wi-zard not li-zard." Her rebuke, of course, triggered a long explanation of how the wizard was really a lizard. She would shake her head in mock seriousness.

There was some method to my madness. I did not want to be posi-tioned in her mind as the feared disciplinarian. Yes, I was ultimately responsible for the discipline, but there was no way I was going to be positioned as "the bad guy."

Besides, I was having too much fun. I was able to release my "inner comedian." My "inner singer" soared.

What could possibly be more fun than laughter between father and daughter?

Even if you don't always feel it, give her a smile. Let her know how wonderful life is by the joy and laughter you create with her.

Have fun with her. These will be among your very best memories.

55

Find the Funny

There is nothing worse than an embarrassing parent. Especially when you're a teenager. There were a few instances when my dad embarrassed me so badly that I wished the heavens would open up and flood the county leaving no survivors.

Twice he really went out of his way to embarrass me. I don't know why, but he did. One of those times had something to do with a large beef stick from Hickory Farms. With it, he challenged me to a duel. I was thirteen. The mall was full of holiday shoppers.

I couldn't speak I was so angry with him. What if I knew people? What if someone from school was there? What would I do then?

I wasn't one of those girls who could easily shrug off an incident like that. I desperately wanted to fit in with my peers.

I really, really, really wanted to be the cool girl. I wanted to go to the overnight parties over the weekend and the local LDS Church on Sunday (though I wasn't particularly religious, nor even a Mormon) and then be able to talk about our Lord Jesus Christ (and the Simpsons) every Monday morning before Home Room started. But it just wasn't to be. Not with my dad around. He never took my concerns for popularity too seriously.

So there we were, in the middle of the mall and I hear an "en garde". For a minute I just stood there hoping that this was some sort of psychotic break I was having and it wasn't real. I looked around to see other fathers glancing in amused fascination at my dad.

I did what any normal, average American teenager would do. I walked away pretending that I had no relation to the crazy person with the beef stick.

He called out to me swinging the meat, and I continued walking quickly in the opposite direction, hoping I would be lucky enough that I wouldn't run into anyone that I knew.

He had to hustle to catch up with me, guffawing over the fact that he had just embarrassed me so badly.

I didn't think I would ever speak to him again. But there were still errands to run.

57

This embarrassment went on for some time, my dad taking extreme pleasure in embarrassing me.

However, all is not lost because I found a way to train a father out of this disgusting habit. There are two phases to the training.

The first phase is to say something that he would find embarrassing. Say it out loud, directly to him. For my dad, the mere mention of sex and me (regardless of whether or not I was having it) would shut him up immediately and bring him back under control.

So it could go something like this:

Dad picks up large beef stick. "En garde".

Daughter takes a moment to study the beef stick, then VERY casually compares that to her boyfriend. "Wow, that kind of reminds me of Bob."

Dad takes a moment to digest what Daughter has just said and very quietly puts the beef stick away lest she say anything else.

Obviously, this is an extreme example, but there it is. By training your father this way, it eliminates the need to completely disassociate yourself from him as he will think twice before he intentionally (or unintentionally) tries to embarrass you.

Just keep in mind that there is humor and then there is just plain mean. Avoid "The Mean" (even, and most especially, when you really want to strike him down) and find the funny. It's a better strategy than anything else and you <u>both</u> will learn from the experience!

Once you have gotten the first phase in and he is a little more careful about what he does, then you start to work in the second phase of training.

This is where it gets really fun. This is where your dad and you each start looking for the humor in any situation.

The beef stick for example. He tried to pull that one on me again a few years back. Being much more comfortable in my skin than I was back then, I decided to play along. I picked up my own beef stick and proceeded to fence with him until we were scolded by the Hickory Farms employee.

We laughed so hard that I thought I might pee in my pants. (I didn't, but it was a close call.) There was such ridiculous humor in how we were behaving and since we were willing to go the distance, we both had fun and provided a few laughs for some other harried Christmas shoppers.

Today I bait him about my still being a "virgin" several times over at this point. Or I'll make up stories of sexual escapades that go on and on and on, just to see his reaction. It's totally hilarious to watch him react.

We are weird and some people will probably think that our relationship is too open, but you can't help but appreciate the humor of it all. In fact, when we start this banter, it is very common for others to join in the fray.

So the rule: Find the Funny.

It'll take the pressure off the serious.

Buy Her What She Wants

One obvious way kids learn is by having *stuff to play with*..

You will read very shortly about Jenny "drip marketing" her dad to get something.

For me, the fun part was being dripped on because, you see, I had decided somewhere along the way to just buy her whatever she wanted. I could afford it, and she took such care to ease me into the store I couldn't do otherwise.

I probably would not have made that decision if she wanted the whole store, but she didn't. She would actually think out very carefully what she wanted. It was the "Baby Doll" or whatever. And as you will see, she had a whole routine to get it

I loved the routine and possibly made her work just a little harder than she might otherwise have had to work had I not seen what she was doing.

But, Dad, think about this. By letting her routine work, I was empowering her. Wasn't I? She had learned how to control this big, occasionally scary guy at the center of her life. She knew by doing what I wanted, I would do what she wanted.

Was Jenny manipulating me with her "First get him in the store" routine? You bet. With smiles, treats and cooperation. Who wouldn't want to be manipulated like that? It worked every time. Still does twenty odd years later.

Buy Me Something!

Now this is a rule that should not be taken too seriously, as it is only in fun, as we all know that money cannot, under any circumstances, buy love.

HOWEVER! It can bring a lot of joy to a little girl who misses her father, and vice versa.

When I was little and my daddy was often away on business, it was hard to deal with. I missed him a lot. But there was one thing I could always count on when he was away.

When he came home, he would always bring magical gifts of what was to me untold fortune that made up for the time that he was away.

Mostly they were little things, but things that I loved. He brought me pretty plastic bags, because I loved to pack my underwear in little bags and hide them all over the house. (Figure that one out!) Bags from a department store, or the airport, or wherever he had been. Simple things, that didn't cost much, but brought me so much pleasure that I still remember the excitement I felt as he pulled out a pretty bag.

He once brought me a pelican feather he had found on a Florida beach, and I still have it today. It makes a lovely fountain pen.

For the jokingly rude things that he says to press my buttons, for the times that I don't get to see him, or that he is out of town, or has no time for long conversations, I simply say "I shall add it to your bill."

At this point, I think he owes me well into the range of our national debt. But each time I see him, and he pulls out a little trinket, or a bag (as I still love bags and boxes to hide things in), all is forgiven.

The first time I realized the sway that I had over my father's decisions was a revelation of vast proportions.

I had seen this really wonderful, funny plastic dinosaur in a Sinclair gas station. I knew that it would be the most perfect swimming pool toy in the world, and I decided that I must have it and it was very important to my very survival that I own that one object. So I asked my dad casually as we were driving by if we could stop at the gas station for a minute. By the time I was done asking the question we were way past it and too late to go back to that gas station.

So I waited patiently for the next time we passed that gas station. We passed it several times before we finally stopped for gas. So staring at that dinosaur in the window I thought very carefully about what I was going to say to convince him to buy it.

Since I thought the dinosaur was cool, I figured he must not have seen it. Otherwise he would have thought it was just as cool and perhaps purchased one for his very own. I decided to point it out to him so that he could see just how neat it was and how great it would be to have one for a pool toy. Then being his daughter, I could "borrow" it. That was my childish philosophy at any rate.

So I got him in the store, pointed it out, and told him how much fun he could have floating on it in the pool.

63

He agreed that it would be a great pool toy. End of story. No dinosaur for Jenny.

Hmmm. Time to regroup and rethink the strategy. I decided to gently nudge him every time we drove by that particular gas station. I would just mention casually "Oh. There's that cool dinosaur in the window." And that was all.

I think we probably drove by it once a day, and every so often I would do what modern day salesmen call a "drip campaign", like a leaky faucet that never stops, but never overwhelms, I talked about this dinosaur. Finally, finally, finally, my dad looked over as we approached the gas station and turned in.

He asked me to show him the dinosaur again, which I did, and after explaining the benefits of this great floating creature, I walked out of that gas station with my prize.

That was the discovery I made, the beginnings of a great rule: First get him in the store.

As I got older, things became more expensive than my five-dollar dinosaur, so I added extra steps to the original strategy, as follows:

Step 1

First, go to the store, or the mall, or whatever, without your father and carefully select the item that you want to have. Planning is everything here.

It is important in this step not to go overboard. Select one, maybe two items that you really want to have. (If you go overboard and pick out a hundred things, or something that is way beyond his ability to pay for, you are just setting yourself up for disappointment.) The idea is to find something he can afford and you would love to have.

My usual thing would be a little outfit with matching belt or earrings, or something like that.

Step 2

Add up the price without tax, of course, so that when you present him with what you have picked out you can go right into the pitch.

Step 3

Suggest an outing with your father. A drive perhaps.

Very Important: *Do not tell him that you want him to buy something for you.*

Step 4

Take him on the route that goes by the store. When you see the store ahead, suggest you stop because there is something you want him to see. Get him into the store, and browse. Keep the browsing short! But pretend to browse for a few minutes.

65

Step 5

Take his hand, smile at him and say with great enthusiasm, "Come see this really cute outfit that I found."

And then show him and proceed to tell him how this particular outfit will benefit him, should he buy it for you. This is where you tell him how much it costs, mention it briefly but do not dwell on the cost, rather the benefits of having this particular item.

Step 6

Don't pressure him! But suggest that you should try it on, so that he can see how cute you look in it.

Step 7

Try it on, model it, and change back into your regular clothes. Say to him as you put the thing back on the rack "It's really cute, huh?" And await his answer. Now this step is crucial. Do not ask for it. Do not beg to have it. Do not make silly promises that you cannot keep such as "I will never ask for anything ever again." No, no, no. Let him think that he wants to buy it for you to see the bright smile that you would bestow upon him.

Step 8

When he asks you if you want to have this item, smile brightly and nod your head.

At this point, he will take it to the register and pay for it. And you get to take it home.

Step 9

When you get back, immediately show everyone the present that your marvelous daddy just bought for you.

Step 10

A short time later, write him a note, a thank-you, or even draw him a picture, to thank him for his gifts Showing your appreciation for what he does this way will ensure that he continues to do so.

Now this sequence of steps has worked every time from the time I could actually speak.

The only times I have failed at getting my dad to buy me something is when I didn't get him into the store so that he could see my enthusiasm for the item he was about to spend hard earned money on.

An important thing to remember with this particular rule is never ever pressure your dad into buying something. You let him decide to buy it, because you are so enthusiastic about it.

Daddies can never resist their little girl's happiness. You show him that happiness, and he will walk on water to give you anything.

His reward will be the brightness that only daughters can bring.

I promise you this, if you make him feel good by smiling at him and laughing in pleasure, there will be nothing you ask for that he won't provide.

67

Pick Your Rules

I think it is a huge mistake, in life, relationships, country, business or whatever to have a lot of rules.

A child especially, cannot think about dozens or hundreds of things he or she must do or can't do. (It works for adults too. There are, after all, only ten commandments, not 507.)

But I also believe that the ones you impose should be followed by swift, certain justice.

I never threatened or yelled. Jenny knew absolutely for certain the penalties for violating the few rules I had imposed.

Most likely, this opinion was burned into my mind while attending grad school at the University of Virginia.

"The University," as those of us who went there still call it, has an honor code written by Thomas Jefferson.

It is one sentence long.

"A Gentleman does not lie, cheat or steal."

There was one punishment: Expulsion. Students as well as professors were honor bound to enforce it.

Had I seen another student cheating—which I never did—I was honor bound to confront the offending student and say, "I saw you cheating. You have 24 hours to leave the University."

If the cheater chose, he or she could just pack up and leave the University, and no one would ever know why. Or the student could appeal to the Honor Committee.

But for liars, cheaters, and thieves, there was no mercy, extenuating circumstances, or plea bargaining.

Guilty = Gone.

So the honor code focused on what was truly important.

69

Interestingly, with that code enforced, life at the University was extraordinarily free. In the middle of an exam, if I wanted to take a break, I just got up and walked out. There was no question that I might be cheating. No one followed me. There were no "bathroom monitors."

It was the wonderful freedom I enjoyed at the University of Virginia that lead me to the conclusion: Don't make a whole lot of rules, Dad. Go for the important stuff...like the truth. And enforce it.

So I decided that Jenny would have absolute certainty that if she broke the few rules we set, known consequences would be handed out.

There was absolutely no confusion over possible exceptions, wiggle room, going to her Mom for mercy.

If she broke Dad's rules, Dad administered the justice.

Because the rules were simple to understand, few in number, and the punishments certain, we never wound up focused on the "Don'ts."

In looking back, "Don't Ever Lie to Me" was my equivalent of Mr. Jefferson's honor code for daughters. I understood that if I knew the truth, I could solve any other problem or difficulty life might throw at us. If there was a "drop dead" rule, that was it.

Without the truth, I knew I would attempt to solve wrong problems. These solutions would, by definition, be wrong solutions.

So I needed the truth.

When Jenny was about five, she presented me with a marvelous opportunity to teach her this. She has already told it to you from her side. Here's my version and why I did it.

One day, I asked her to take the dog outside to go potty. She came right back inside. Hmmmm. We went outside together and, as you know, she told a really stupid lie.

I decided it was time for The Lesson.

After visiting the crime scene, I took her upstairs.

We sat down on the bed and I put her on my lap.

I carefully explained that she was never to tell me a lie and that every time I caught her, she would get a spanking.

I then turned her over my knee, and swatted her about as hard as one would hit a pillow to make a place for one's head.

She sobbed mightily.

At this point, many readers will be up in arms about brutality, beatings or whatever else you imagine I did to "innocent" Jenny.

That's not it. At age five, children may not be able to comprehend the verbal statement, "If you ever lie to me again, I will spank you."

Jenny did understand, "If you do this again, SPANK, I will do it again. You don't do it. I won't do it."

She got that.

That was the only spanking I ever gave her, not because she never lied again but because of a second rule regarding confession. It was, however, the certainty that I would enforce Rule #1 that made Rule #2 work.

Rule #2 said, "If you confess before I find out you lied, you will not get spanked."

OK, Dad, now listen up.

What I was really trying to teach was not "Don't lie." I was trying to teach the virtue of truth-telling. Telling the truth, even when confessing a lie, was rewarded by no spanking, and even forgiveness, with no punishment.

Because you are part of your daughter's life, because you communicate with her and observe her, you will notice telltale signs she has lied about something.

There's the furtive look, the "taking too long to answer the question", the flush to the cheeks when confronted with a possible offense.

You don't want to nail her necessarily and immediately administer out The Punishment. You want to give her the opportunity to confess because by so doing she grows.

So whenever I would catch the contradiction or downcast eye, I might say something like, "Jenny, is there anything I need to know?"

She learned very quickly to confess because I only spanked her that once.

There was actually one other time other time I caught her in a lie, and when she confessed, I instantly forgave her.

At about age 13, she had asked me for some money to go to a local amusement park, which I gave her. Joava later mentioned she had given Jenny some money, miraculously the same amount. Hmmm.

"Jenny, its confession time. Why did you do that?"

She burst into tears and told me that her little friend's dad had died. They were having a hard time financially, and she wanted to take her to the amusement park and was afraid I wouldn't give her the money. We both had a good cry and I gave her extra money.

The only other rule that could have resulted in The Spanking was, "Don't ever swear in front me."

I hate a trash mouth. I grew up in the South and was taught to say "Yes, Sir" and "No, Sir" to my dad.

After hearing some of Jenny's little friends come out with some pretty awful streams of profanity, I knew the opportunity was close at hand.

One day about age 6 or so, we were outside in the yard on a pretty spring day, and Jenny let fly with one of my least favorite words.

This word might be called a multi-tasking word because it can be used as a noun, verb, adverb or adjective.

I grabbed her by the wrist and marched her into the house. We went into the bathroom. I put the lid down on the toilet, sat down and put her on my lap.

"Jenny," I said, "There is something dirty in your mouth. That's why those filthy words came out. If you ever swear in front of me again, your only choice will be: Do you want me to wash that dirt out of your mouth with liquid soap or bar soap? Do we understand each other completely?"

Eyes wide, she nodded her head.

The second time she swore in front of me she was in her twenties.

Why the big deal?

Partly just my own dislike of foul language. But partly to teach self-control.

Did Jenny swear?

You bet. On occasion, her older sister would whisper, "I heard Jenny say...."

But not in front of me. She had total certainty that I would wash her mouth out with soap, which I would. I never did.

The rule was not: "Don't swear."

It was, "Don't swear in front of me."

And by the way, to this day she doesn't swear very much in front me. She knows I don't like it and respects that.

OK, so let's deal with the S word—sex.

73

Should you have rules galore, endless harangues, and lectures?

No.

You have three lines of defense against the most powerful force in the world.

The first line is (you guessed it), be #1.

As #1, of course you talk, talk, talk, educate, educate, educate. Be involved, involved, involved, in her life.

As #1, you are, of course, threatened by the boys that come around. They're the young bears trying to take down the old bear.

They will come around. You actually want them around, just not too close. By being with boys, she will learn to make her own choices. But the boys who come around must be given notice that they are on Poppa Bear's turf and the penalty for staying too long is awful. You will learn all about that in my later chapter, "Boys Are the Enemy." It's how to keep the buggers off balance without forcing The Daughter to defend them.

Your third line of defense assumes the first two crumble and she does have sex while she is under your care and protection.

Now the game becomes: Make sure she's unpregnant and disease free.

When Jenny was about 15, I read an article about a woman who had a condom in her purse when she was attacked by a rapist. She actually convinced the rapist to wear the condom. In that same time period, I had also read or seen something about condom earrings. That's right *condom earrings*. What a horrible product! I promptly talked to Jenny about them and suggested I pick up a pair for her to wear.

She was completely grossed out.

But look what I was doing. I was working on my second line of defense. This was just another way of staying on message: "If you do it, I expect you to use birth control."

I went so far as to teach her about condoms.

I showed her one. I took one out of its package and explained how to put one on a boy if she should decide to have sex.

Did it work?

She never had an STD, never got pregnant.

Pick Your Battles

There is something to be said about the differences between a man and woman; or, in our case, a father and a daughter.

I like tattoos and body piercing, whereas my dad grew up in the forties and fifties when piercing your ears was scandalous and tattoos were for those "unmentionable people" who don't mingle with "good" families.

He can listen to Mozart for hours, while I prefer Eminem and the Glam Rock Hair Bands of the 80s.

I like tanks, tight hoodies and low-slung jeans that show my tattoo when I bend over. This gives my father heart palpitations since he would rather I wear neck-to-toe draperies.

And yet beneath all these differences there is an understanding between us that - though I am his daughter - I am my own individual.

On the clothing issue alone we could probably argue for countless days, making each other miserable, neither one willing to see the other's viewpoint.

I am sure that my dad wishes I'd never gotten my tattoo or my belly button pierced. I am sure he'd prefer I'd kept to just the simple piercing in my earlobes rather than the cartilage pierced in my upper ear.

But at the end of the day, what I do to my own body is my own choice. If I want to tattoo every inch of skin, then that is my choice and my right.

We could fight about it for sure. No question, but we don't because it's not important and a waste of oxygen. I'm going to do what I am going to regardless of whether or not I have my dad's approval and he knows that. I've always been that pig-headed and stubborn and I am aware of that. However, because we don't nit-pick every action or thought, it has given those "serious" talks we've had that much more importance on both sides.

There is a version of this rule aptly called "Pick Your Battles" that floats around every so often, but if you do this right, there is no battle.

And that's better all around.

77

The Father's Guiding Principle: Boys Are the Enemy

As a former boy, I can attest that about age twelve, boys stop looking at little girls as merely annoying creatures who can't pitch or hit and begin looking at them as objects of sexual conquest.

It is The Father's responsibility to put so many obstacles in the road that the headlong rush to seduce The Daughter is diverted, delayed, and where necessary, forbidden until your daughter is old enough to make her own decisions. That age is 39.

Before I reveal my secrets to all, I do want to relay a story of the point at which The Father gives up his #1 position.

After too many years of not being #1 with Nicci, my oldest daughter, I earned that position only after her first marriage broke up. I earned it with help, support and encouragement through tough times.

With no other man in her life at the time, I came through.

In November 2001, she married a wonderful young man. My wife and I totally approved.

Following the wedding ceremony, as Father of the Bride I, of course, proposed a toast.

"Devin," I said, "In a perfect world, a father is the #1 man in his daughter's life until the day she gets married. But when that day arrives, the father must give up that position to her husband. So, in addition to proposing a toast to Nicci and you, I would like to formally present you with my number."

With that, I presented Devin with a wallet-size, laminated card that said simply "#1."

"In your family group," I continued, "you are now the # 1 man in Nicci's life. It is appropriate that you have my card. Justin her son, and my grandson, is #2. And I am extremely proud to become #3 in the Stokes family hierarchy."

With the birth of their son Lucas, I am now the #4 man in my daughter's life.

Now that you know at which point you must give up #1, let's talk about a variety of ways to use it—and not use it—during teen-age years.

Surely there is a law of physics that applies here: "For every action there is an equal but opposite reaction."

Aggressively oppose your daughter's choice, and she must aggressively defend.

So here are some ways to keep the boys off balance.

Assign him a number

When Jenny was in her later teens, she became enamored with a young man in whose presence I detected a waft of rodentia. (He *was* a rat.) But at her age, there's nothing a dad can do, right? She can make her own decisions, right? Wrong. Until she is *married*, you're still #1. You just better be clever.

We were at a horseshow. Jenny was with The Rodent. I was walking with our son, Bret. Jenny ran up in between the two of us and asked, "How are my two favorite men?"

The sky opened. Inspiration struck.

With Jenny right there, I turned to Bret. "I am the # 1 man in her life, correct?"

"Correct," Bret correctly responded.

"You, as the older brother, are #2. Correct?"

"Damn right," Bret correctly responded.

"Does this mean he is #3?" I asked.

Bret thought about it and said, "No, that's much too high a number."

"So, obviously," I said, "as Numbers One and Two in her life, it is our responsibility to assign various suitors a number."

After much discussion, we agreed on # 73. We so informed the couple and indicated we would reconsider raising The Rodent's number in five years.

After intense lobbying by The Daughter, we agreed to raise The Rodent's number to 49 and would only consider a review of that status if a $5,000, non-refundable re-application fee were submitted.

Now what did I do here?

I let her know I did not approve. But I didn't make such a big deal out of it that she had to defend him. I was strong enough as #1 to make it stick. Soon his number was reduced to 7 trillion. Then we had a formal de-numbering ceremony. Whew! Another one bites the dust.

Present her with clothing to wear on a date

Once when pondering some suitor or other, I decided The Daughter needed more suitable clothing to wear on a date.

Who else better to design such clothing than The Father?

So I got to work.

I found a scowling picture of me in a tux. I ironed that on the front of the shirt along with the words, "I'm her dad. Don't even think about it."

On the back, I found a picture of a wolf dog's head, also scowling. The back said, "I'm her dog. Ditto."

I thought that was a terrific idea, but as I recall, Jenny no more wore it than she would have worn a garbage bag.

But once again, I delivered the message, this time to her.

"Don't even think about it."

Jenny's current suitor is #38. I like him a lot. One day, I might even give up my number to him. (Whoops. Poor guy. Lost his number. Sorry pal, you ain't getting my number!)

Give him the "DAD Checklist" (Dads Against Dating)

This form, which you will see shortly and can download from our website, is my masterpiece. We've posted it in MS Word form so you can customize it at your pleasure.

81

I designed it when The Rodent was going to come up for Thanksgiving. It was time for some atomic fire power.

When I wrote it, I assumed no one had ever thought of this idea before.

But one night, I had gone to the airport to do a complicated ticket for overseas travel. I went late in the evening so I could have the undivided attention of the ticket agent.

While I was talking to her, two airline workers nearby, a man and woman, were laughing to the point of tears.

When I was done with my ticket, I went over to them, "OK, guys," I said, "What's so funny?"

The guy showed me a "Checklist for Getting a Date," that he had written for his daughter.

82

He had some things on his checklist I didn't have, which I immediately added to mine.

So out of a very basic desire to protect one's daughter, we had independently conceived the idea of letting a kid know, "Don't touch my daughter."

Over the years, I've probably seen four or five checklists, all accomplishing with humor and style what too many fathers try to do with force and threat.

P.S. Yes, I did give it to The Rodent. He actually handled himself quite well. But I knew the message had been delivered.

The DAD (Dads Against Dating) Checklist

Checklist For:

_____

(Insert Name of Innocent Daughter Here)

This Checklist may be initiated at the request of The Daughter, but preferably, by a member of the Suitor Committee for Approval Tomorrow (SCAT) when a likely candidate presents himself for a date.

The Father's Duties

Fathers do not, by their nature, approve of the modern dating system. They would much prefer arranged marriages with virgin sons from families of known reputation.

In the absence of this much saner system, The Father and other SCAT members assume the responsibility to help The Daughter pick a suitable husband by using his and their vast skills (and memories of what it was like to be a boy) to root out unsuitable candidates.

Fathers have very broad powers and may reject The Candidate for any reason shown below or other reasons that become evident or for no reason.[1]

This petition to SCAT will be rejected immediately unless accompanied by the following documentation:[2]

----

1. Acceptance: The application may only be approved after all steps have been meticulously followed. It may, however, be rejected for any reason.
2. The applicant must assemble the required information and _mail_ it to The Father. DO NOT present your person with the information. That would annoy The Father and would cause him to immediately reject the application.

Background Information

Statement from your dentist that you do not suffer from gingivitis or halitosis (which would offend The Father, and, if you ever get close enough, The Daughter)   _____

Three character references from people at least 20 years older than you. Suggestion: Ministers, teachers, and retired bankers   _____

Letters of reference from three previous girlfriends attesting to the fact that you do not own chest jewelry (cause for immediate disqualification)   _____

A recent photo   _____

Notarized statement from insurance agent attesting to your flawless driving record   _____

Unedited video clip of a walk-around of your car

(Designed to detect that it is not a van, station wagon or SUV. Also designed to detect traces of bumper stickers, one of which might read "If it's a rockin' don't come knocking".

Should either be detected, the former applicant should RUN, preferably in a zigzag fashion.)   _____

84

The Father reviews the written application. Where the qualifications of The Candidate do not unduly offend the father, he schedules a personal interview.

Disqualifiers

Ask The Applicant the following:[1]

Do you own a truck or van?

Does it have a waterbed or mattress in the back?

Do you own a waterbed?

Do you own condoms?

Do you own pornography?

Do you have an earring, nose ring, belly-button ring?

Tattoo? (On what?)

The Father makes small talk with The Applicant and determines the following:

Applicant's sense of humor is amusing and personality is pleasant enough not to annoy The Father   _____

Can discuss current affairs intelligently   _____

Does not appear to be a communist, feminist or drug addict   _____

Appearance does not offend The Father   _____

After a sniff check, The Father decides whether to allow the application to continue and initials one of the following:

_____ Disapproved!   _____   Approval to Continue This Form

If approved: Forward entire package to The Grandfather or Moral Authority.

1. Wrong answers to the Disqualifiers immediately terminate the interview.

The Moral Authority

Duties include asking subtle questions to determine if The Applicant is someone we want to be in the same general vicinity as The Daughter.

Suggested Subtle Questions:

What church do you attend? How often do you attend?

_____

What would be the best time to interview your mother, father, minister?

_____

I'm going to give you some hypothetical situations.[1] Just tell me the first word that comes to mind:

If I were in an accident, the last thing I would want injured is my:

_____

If I were beaten, the last bone I would want broken is my:

_____

The one thing I hope this application does not ask me is:

_____

What do you want to be if you grow up?

_____

Condoms come in packs of _____?

A woman's place is in the: _____

1. I can't take credit for all the questions here. Somewhere along the way I saw these on one of those emails that whiz around the Internet. These "moral authority" questions are in at least 1220 web docs. They were too good to pass up.

When I meet a girl, the first thing I notice about her is:

_____

(If this begins with "T" or "A", discontinue. Leave at once. Running in a serpentine fashion is recommended.)

What is the current rate on a hotel room?

_____

If applicant passes to this point, the Moral Authority then determines The Applicant has:

Profound knowledge of world religions _____

Has read _Gone with the Wind_ and _Atlas Shrugged_ 10-15 times each _____

In the unlikely event The Applicant has made it this far, the Moral Authority has The Candidate recite from memory:

87

The names of all Fred Astaire movies _____

The speeches given at his last three family reunions _____

In the likely event the application is not approved, The Applicant is notified with a letter detailing his shortcomings and suggesting there might be less vigilant fathers elsewhere. The letter thoughtfully recommends joining one of the priestly orders. No appeal will be accepted.

_____Disapproved! _____ Approval to Continue This Form

If approved: In the unlikely event the petition has been approved, The Applicant is advised to travel (at his own expense) for a meeting with The Brother or other Approved Expert on the Manly Arts for further examination of his suitability to have a date with The Daughter.

The Expert on the Manly Arts

The candidate spends a day with The Brother or other Expert on the Manly Arts. The Father is only interested in MANLY candidates as suitors for The Daughter.

The Brother reviews The Candidate's collection of movies and books. He is expected to have copies of all of Arnold's movies and, of course, those featuring "The Rock." (The Father will be most interested to learn that any copy of the movie "Junior" is unopened as a manly man would not be interested in a movie or any other information about a pregnant Arnold.)

Takes The Candidate to the gym

10 mile run: Beginning Pulse _____ Ending Pulse: _____

1 mile swim: Beginning Pulse _____ Ending Pulse: _____

Bench press: _____lbs _____reps
If less than 200 pounds, discontinue application.

Squat: _____lbs _____reps

Takes The Candidate to "All You Can Eat" buffet. Must demonstrate substantial appetite.   _____

Survival Skills

Takes The Candidate into nearby desert or wilderness area and leaves candidate with flat tire, no gas and no money. The Candidate must return car in working order in 8 hours.

At this point, The Brother casually discusses family hair loss. Depending on the preferences of The Daughter (one of the few allowed), this may or may not be a disqualifying feature.

The Brother inconspicuously inspects The Candidate's gums and ears. Samples The Candidate's breath at least four times during the week.

The Brother engages The Candidate in conversation on the subject of "Dating Manners" and another on the exact meaning, history, etymology of the phrase, "Do not..."

The Brother inspects photos of baseball hat collection. (Look carefully to determine if any show distortions in their natural shape that might have come from being worn sideways.) The Father does not like this.

The Brother must spend enough time with The Candidate to determine he does not have excessive chest hair showing. Tufts of back hair are immediate disqualifiers.

Through personal inspection, verifies that The Candidate does not have long nose or ear hair.

89

_____Disapproved! _____ Approval to Continue This Form

If The Candidate has not been disqualified by The Brother, this Disqualification Form and all attachments are forwarded to the Chair-MAN of the Suitor Committee for Approval Tomorrow (who is, naturally The Father.)

Notification

The Father notifies The Candidate he has passed this modest checklist and may now go on one DATE to a suitable location arranged by The Father. Four Members of SCAT will accompany The Candidate and The Daughter. Candidate will, of course, pay all expenses. (The Brother likes Lobster.)

So as not to intimidate The Candidate and The Daughter, SCAT members will remain silent on the date, only taking notes to be discussed further. SCAT members will pay special attention to the time The Candidate brings The Daughter home.

Findings and Recommendations

Disapproved!

Approved

The Committee, having met in full executive session, has examined The Candidate and found him NOT WORTHY of The Daughter.

The Candidate is rejected and may only reapply upon payment of a $5000 re-application fee whose sole purpose is to compensate SCAT Members for their annoyance at having to deal with The Candidate again.

The Committee having met in full has examined The Candidate and found him acceptable to date The Daughter. The Candidate is now assigned a number by The Committee for convenience of referring to him. (The Father is #1.)

A suitable number for The Suitor could be #73 to indicate his standing in The Daughter's life.

For convenience sake, The Candidate may be referred to by his number should future oral or written communication be required. This status is subject to periodic examination and may be upgraded in five years.

Status is petitionable by The Daughter.

The Daughter's Guiding Principle:
Workarounds!

Fathers are funny.

For some reason they think that just because they were rowdy horn-dogs as teenagers, every boy between 2 and 92 is the same way.

The funniest part about it all is that girls (especially teenage girls) are just as sexually fixated as dudes. It's just not as, shall we say, obvious. We can hide it better.

The Hormone Season begins when we embark upon puberty. I am not sure when it ends. I'll let you know. However, in the midst of all the thoughts about sex are the desires for true love, and weeding through the lies and come-ons can be a bit of a joke.

In fact, it has become a bit of a running gag between my dad and me—one of those jokes revolves around a certain kind of top I favor that displays the "breastual region" (as I like to call it). I wear the shirt and he starts looking for the old Poncho we got in Tijuana when I was nine. This leads me into my next joke about baiting the hook for one of those many fish in the sea.

On and on it goes leading both down the road to hysterical laughter.

Who would have thought that there was so much humor to be had with my dad when it came to sex? Not me. But it is hilarious.

You've read the Disqualification Form at this point, so you have a good idea of how my father's brain malfunctions. What he failed to mention is that I actually present this form to my dates.

I figure that any guy who gets offended or put off by this isn't for me, because obviously he has no sense of humor.

The guy that does this form and does it with just as much fun as my dad had writing it, will be the guy that I marry. It's as simple as that.

But as a teenager, it's a little hard to get around these viewpoints that The Father may have about The Boyfriend.

By the time I started dating, he was well versed in the "You Touch Her, You Die" lecture. He was also very familiar by how non-threatening that was to young men in my generation. So, on that point, he had to re-strategize.

What he didn't count on, though, was that I wanted my dad's opinion on the guy I was dating. I wanted him to fit in with my family and their opinion was very important to me.

And so I sought it out. I just didn't think his opinion would be as bad as it was.

I had been dating my guy for about a month when I finally introduced him to my dad. You know the story. He was assigned a number.

I lobbied hard to get his number raised. The highest he managed to get was 43. Without doing anything other than giving him this number, it told me everything.

And yet it also told me that there was hope. His number could go up. Obviously, things had to change in some way.

They did. We broke up. He was de-numbered.

For every guy I've dated, my dad has assigned a number effectively showing me how much he likes or dislikes them.

On occasion, when the number is VERY low, those relationships didn't last much beyond getting that assignment. Usually this was because the man in question didn't have the kind of humor that fit well with my family.

I do have a strange family. We are a wild and crazy bunch of opinionated individuals.

Eventually, the entire family will get on the numbering bandwagon, which is now an amusing activity during the holidays.

My nephew will address presents to my brother-in-law using the number system. From my brother-in-law to my dad. It goes on and on. But only the males are numbered. The females, we get to keep our names. Until we're married.

Anyway, enough about those weirdos.

My dad never interfered with my relationships, and he certainly supported everything I did, but I always knew if he didn't like the boy, more often than not, he was absolutely right in his intuition.

So while he threatens, and grunts, and chases away the boys who come calling, it will make it that much sweeter when I can finally manage to bring home someone he *does* approve of.

I have gone through certain phases in my life when the only thing I wanted was to get married as soon as possible. I was about 12 or 13 and my goal was to be married by the ripe old age of eighteen, and have my first child by the age of twenty.

By the time I turned eighteen the thought of getting married gave me the creeps and I couldn't imagine *ever* being married. I was very enchanted with being a sperm-donored single mother, or living with a boyfriend, and having kids together that way. You know, a very modern, twenty-first century kind of relationship. My anti-marriage campaign developed into a theory that marriage was actually the biggest conspiracy around.

Much to my father's pleasure, though, I have now outgrown that phase, and the thought of getting married and sharing my life with someone who shares my own passions and interests is very appealing to me.

So after a (short) string of boyfriends, dates and whatnots, I began to learn through my experience that, strangely enough, I found myself looking for someone who was like my father.

Now, don't get all Freudian on me, because there is something to be said about a father setting a good example of honor and chivalry to prove that all men actually aren't pigs. And being that a girl's first male contact usually comes from her father, it goes to prove that there is some truth to a girl's choosing a man very much like her dad.

The qualities that I observe in my own parent's marriage are something that I want for myself. I see a lot of my mother and my father in my own mannerisms and attitude, and I know I look for those character definitions in a partner.

Their example has been 30-some odd years of a solid, sane relationship that tells me that marriages can actually work in a day and age when the percentage of divorce is higher than the percentage of lasting marriages

When I got through my "Marriage is a conspiracy" phase, I began searching for a man who would be a good husband and, more importantly, a good father. You see, I have reverted to the more traditional way of thinking that two parents, married, sharing their lives together are a very important factor in the raising of a family. I was lucky enough to have both my parents together through thick and thin. By those standards, I believe that my children should deserve the same. I owe it to them.

So I found myself looking for a man that would be as good to the children I would like to have as my father was to me and my brother and sister. I want a man very much like my father, who is willing to work as hard as I will to provide for my family.

So I guess the only real workaround is to bring home someone he'll like.

Déjà vu

Was it last year or perhaps the year before,
You held my pinky as we walked round the block?
Yes, I think it was just a month ago,
I rested my hand on your head,
And joked that you were just the right height.

Last week, Yes, I think that's when it was,
I walked down the beach,
Spied a feather.
She'll love that, I thought.
You did.
I think it was just a few months ago, I told you,
"Jenny, use your magic and make the snow disappear."
You said, "But I don't have any magic."
To which I replied, "Then why, when you're around, do people feel
so much better?"
"Dad," you said, "That's not magic, that's love."
Yes, I'm sure that was just last winter, or maybe yesterday.

Yesterday, last year or many years ago,

It matters not at all,

For love is above, beyond

Even outside of time.

What matters most

Is that special bond

Of father to daughter,

Parent to child,

Adult to adult,

But most of all,

Father to daughter.

Déjà vu

Something today

I've been there before,

And I'm here now.

You have brought great joy to my life, Daughter.

I know that in your life you will bring great joy to many.

You do have the magic.

Love,

Dad

To My Dad

Dear Dad,

As we near the completion of our book, I am a little sad that this project will be ending soon.

Do you remember writing the magical flower? How much fun that was. I still remember giggling as we created a flower that blooms only once every 5,000 years. The story might have disappeared from an errant hard-drive, but its magic still lingers in my memory and makes me smile.

I cannot begin to describe how lucky I am to have you as my dad.

You've been everything I've needed in a dad. You've been my biggest fan, my support group, my confidante. You've been my teacher, my mentor, my hero.

You taught me to appreciate the freedom we have in life, and to fight for those who don't have it. You've taught me about honor and respect, and compassion for those less fortunate than I.

I sometimes wonder what sort of person I would have become had it not been for mom and you guiding my steps when I needed so much help, and letting me run when I was on the right track.

You've given me a passion for life that only comes from feeling safe in the world. You've nurtured my abilities, encouraging me to follow my dreams and ignore self-doubt. You've kicked my butt into gear when I needed a good healthy dose of reality.

And most of all, you have loved me as much as I love you.

Trying to put down in words, and discover the upspoken rules for the things that we did has been a most challenging endeavor.

We did do it right, and for that I thank you.

Love,

Jenny

Afterwords

Common Sense Help

In addition to the commonsense help offered in this book, we thought it would be a great idea to set up a forum in which fathers and daughters could help each other.

Since this is a self-help book, we have established a page at Purple Box Press (www.purpleboxpress.com) called "Fathers & Daughters."

There, you will not find psychiatrists, therapists, psychologists or family counselors. You'll just find people like us, sometimes needing a hand, sometimes willing to lend it. We made it with common sense. You can too.

And, sure, fathers can stock up on our "Date Wear" T-shirts, that latest fashion craze designed by a father for his daughter's all-important first date. And while you're at it, you will want to pick up some of our "Don't Even Think About It" T-shirts. Wear one of these, Dad, and you won't even need to give Lecture #1 to the prospective boy friend. The pictures are worth several thousand words of lecture and harangue. After seeing the father in full regalia, should the suitor come back for a second date, you can download your own copy of our "DAD Checklist" and go to work. You've read it here and, we hope, enjoyed a belly laugh or two. But make sure you get the message behind the laughs.

So, take all this advice as you see fit. The authors ask only that you keep in mind while reading this book that these rules began when The Father heard those special words that instantly and eternally wrapped his world around the tiniest finger:

"Mr. Good, you have a daughter."

The Authors' Credentials and Other Stuff

The authors profess no training, experience or knowledge in self-help, love doctoring, family counseling, psychotherapy, crystal healing, shaman rain dancing, yoga, meditation, mediation, or channeling. (The Father does assert he can channel dogs, accurately perceiving and reporting what they are thinking... but that's another story.)

What we do know with utmost certainty is the path we walked is one you can follow also. The reward is a life-long relationship that forever preserves the magic of daddy and his little girl. Roles do certainly change, but the magic that comes from squeals of delight, butterfly kisses, hands-held, hugs-and-kisses given never fades.

Acknowledgement

The authors each would like to acknowledge a debt of gratitude to L. Ron Hubbard. In The Father's case, much of what he learned about the importance of communication, healthy living and morality, he learned from Mr. Hubbard.

In The Daughter's case, she took a marvelous Hubbard course that helped her find her mission in life.